NEVER SAY YES TO A STRANGER

NEVER SAY YES TO A STRANGER

WHAT YOUR CHILD MUST KNOW TO STAY SAFE

Susan Newman

Photographs by GEORGE TIBONI

A PERIGEE BOOK

This book is a preventive aid to help keep children safe. It can serve as an effective
tool in educating your child, however it is not a guarantee.

Perigee Books
are published by
The Putnam Publishing Group
200 Madison Avenue
New York, NY 10016

Designed by Rhea Braunstein

Library of Congress Cataloging in Publication Data

Newman, Susan, date.
  Never say yes to a stranger.

  Summary: Stories illustrated with photographs depict
different situations in which children are approached
by strangers and explain the importance of understanding
the dangers of such encounters.
  1. Children and strangers—Juvenile literature.
[1. Strangers. 2. Child molesting] I. Tiboni,
George, ill. II. Title.
HQ784.S8N49 1985   362.7'044   84-22698
ISBN 0-399-51114-8

PRINTED IN THE UNITED STATES OF AMERICA
1 2 3 4 5 6 7 8 9 10

*For Andrew and Richard and every
vulnerable child and concerned parent*

Contents

Author's Note

In 1971 I wrote "Ice Cream Isn't Always Good," a booklet to alert young children to the dangers of strangers. In the intervening years, parents have become increasingly fearful of abduction and molestation. They have sought new ways to protect their children from the malicious strangers who dot our communities. Their requests for more teaching tools and stories like "Ice Cream Isn't Always Good" prompted this sequel.

The would-be abductors pictured throughout *Never Say Yes to a Stranger* are, in real life, concerned and caring parents and friends. They hoped that their portrayals would add to the education and safety of all children. For willingly appearing out of character, they deserve special thanks.

I gratefully acknowledge and thank: the Metuchen, New Jersey, Police Department for its cooperation; Patrolman Ronald Moore for his valuable time and enthusiasm; Fred Cohen, Principal of Moss School in Metuchen, for his support and assistance in executing the photography; Thomas G. Matro, Associate Professor of English, Rutgers University, for his insightful suggestions and expertise in evaluating the manuscript.

A Note to Parents

One Is Too Many

Every parent would prefer to have his child grow up believing that the world is a wonderful, safe place. Today this fantasy is both unrealistic and dangerous. The fact is that children are being abducted and molested by strangers . . . everywhere. Boys as frequently as girls. But there comes a time when your child must be on his own, when you must let go. You can do so with relative confidence only if he is prepared to recognize and handle potentially dangerous situations.

Failure to prepare your child is foolish when the consequences are so enormous, so irrevocable. There is no valid excuse for withholding the knowledge and skills he needs to help short-circuit his own abduction, molestation or murder.

This is not a phase of your child's education that can be left solely to his teachers, religious instructors or activity leaders. Your introduction to stranger dangers won't be his first meeting with this threatening topic. Surely, if he has been exposed to television cartoons and fairy tale monsters, he has been afraid and wondered what he would do if he were cornered or chased.

Never Say Yes to a Stranger was developed to eliminate the fear of the unknown and to ready a child for the real world. Its lessons teach what to expect, how to spot trouble and how to react to ensure one's own welfare. Most importantly, it demonstrates that a child *should* say "no" to adults and *should* question authority when necessary. The model child, who is always polite and who always obeys, is no longer the ideal. This child is, in fact, a perfect victim.

Saying "Don't talk to strangers" is vague and totally inadequate. When this warning is mere words, repeated too frequently, a child tends to add it to his already lengthy list of parental don'ts: Don't eat too much candy, don't run with sharp objects, don't climb trees. The photographically illustrated stories are hypothetical situations a child could encounter. The incidents they dramatize help to perfect his decision-making ability by presenting the ammunition he needs to respond quickly. More importantly, they help a child take the dangerous stranger warning seriously, remove it from the endless list of don'ts and give it special meaning.

It is unfortunate that children must be taught to protect themselves from the criminal element of society that preys on them. Those who learn precaution and prevention techniques will have an emergency reserve to call upon should they need it.

A missing child is every parent's fear, but there are concrete steps you can take to allay that fear and reduce your child's chances of becoming a victim in this national crisis. If only one child were missing in the whole world and he was yours, the number would be too high.

How to Use This Book

To get our message across to children without creating undue anxiety is our most critical aim. You cannot predict how your child will react. The idea that someone would want to hurt her or take her away from you may be both frightening and intriguing to her.

Some children will absorb the material in this book matter-of-factly and calmly; others will need time and endless explanation. A few may joke about, or attempt to brush aside, your concern. Even if your child has had extensive stranger training, it's advisable to read through this book with her the first time so you can respond to any new fears or questions.

You will want to select stories appropriate to your child's age, maturity and amount of unsupervised time. For example, Chapter 1 (No Thanks, Stranger), Chapter 2 (Pick of the Litter) and Chapter 3 (Your Mother Sent Me) can be read to a child of nursery school age, but you would not read Chapter 8 (Jennifer Home Alone) until your child is older and more likely to be in a similar situation.

Each scene drives home "caution" without sermonizing and without traumatizing. Photographs, rather than cartoons or illustrations, make it easier for a child to relate to the scene. The impact and importance of the messages are direct and clear; graphic and lurid details are unnecessary. You will find that the tone of both stories and pictures is not ominous, so that after you have introduced your child to a story, she can review it by herself, with friends or with siblings. Should your child ask for specifics, it is wise to answer questions honestly, but briefly.

No child—be she four or fourteen years old—can absorb the information provided here in one sitting. In your desire to cram vital information into your child, you may find yourself rushing through the text and feeling relieved when she seems to comprehend the characters' options and the guidelines that follow. In actuality, you will probably be overburdening her. You can avoid this by reading through one story at a time, discussing it, watching for reactions, waiting for questions. Stop if you feel your child has had enough.

Use your judgment to establish the best pace for your child, but, at the same time, don't underestimate her ability to grasp what you are telling her or what she is reading. By the age of seven, most children are capable of understanding and using all the precautions outlined in this book. However, don't simply assume that your child knows something; be sure she does. Do you *know* your child can place a long-distance telephone call or do you *think* she can?

If your child is very young and will be exposed only to the first few chapters, be sure *you* read Chapters 11 and 12. As she grows, you can be giving her the tools of safety and an insight into strangers that she will need with her increasing independence. One tip, one small hint, could be the speck of knowledge that saves your child.

Active young children are well known for their short memories. Advice and warnings require repetition from time to time. Acting out the stories with your child and making up others will also underscore messages. Use familiar names and places. As lures, choose items or events your child will find irresistible.

The child who knows how to respond to the often inventive cunning of a stranger has a far better chance of walking away from an incident unscathed.

No Matter What, We Love You

In order to achieve the maximum effectiveness from the material in this book, your child must not only know, but believe in his heart, that you love him and always want him home. Your discussions should be calm, unpressured and loving.

One of the most successful and frequently implemented abductors' ploys is to convince a child that his parents don't really want him or care about him. As you discuss the incidents, counter this craftiness with repeated confirmation of your love: "I could not stand it if you were not here and I didn't know where to find you. You're the most important person in the world to me." Use whatever words are comfortable to express your feelings.

Continual reassurance builds the secure foundation a child requires to respond, "It's not true," no matter how many times a lie about your devotion is reiterated; to say "No" when an incredibly appealing lure is offered. Most children who feel wanted and loved willingly assume the responsibility of safe conduct.

Above all, do not threaten to punish your child if he should slip and become involved with a stranger. As you will note from the descriptions of stranger behavior in Chapter 12, it's quite easy to be deceived by a shrewd stranger. The very idea of abduction is itself sufficiently threatening. Adding the promise of parental anger does not help.

In fact, if you blame your child, who is really the victim, you will confuse him. For your child to be completely "stranger-wise" and to be able to cope in a tough spot, he must have no doubts about who will receive your anger and contempt and about who is really the "bad guy."

Who Is a Stranger? Who Is Not?

Before you begin, it is essential that your child understand who is a stranger and who is not. Unless this differentiation is clear-cut she will remain vulnerable.

Ask your child to tell you what she thinks about strangers. If very young, she is likely to tell you that a stranger is a scruffy person who jumps out of the woods or attacks during the dark of night. An older child may tell you that a stranger is someone she doesn't know. If you accept the dictionary definition, this older child would be correct: "an outsider, a newcomer or foreigner; a person not known or familiar to one."

But when teaching stranger caution, the definition must be more encompassing and your rules about strangers must be distinct and very stringent. One way to help your child discriminate is to ask questions often: Is Aunt Janet a stranger? (No) Is the school crossing guard a stranger? (Yes) A precise explanation is in order: Someone you see every day, even if you know his name, can still be a stranger. You don't know him well enough to have dinner at his house, you don't know where he lives, you don't know his children or any of his friends. He's never been in our house.

As you and your child encounter likely candidates whose stranger status could confuse your child, ask her opinion. This will help fine-tune her judgment. Is the mail carrier a stranger? The school bus driver? An activity leader? The man who works in the toy store? It's conceivable that your child will argue that Ben, the elevator operator in your apartment building, is not a stranger because "he gives me a stick of gum every day."

Clarify misconceptions: these "sort-of-know" people are strangers when she is out alone or with friends. It's perfectly okay to have polite exchanges with them—"Hi, beautiful day"— but if they offer to take her somewhere or to give her a gift, she must say "No thanks."

INTRODUCTION
Never Say Yes to a Stranger

When you were a baby, staying safe was easy. Your parents watched over you. They took care of you *all* the time. Now it's up to you. You want to go places with your friends, get to and from school or go downtown without your parents tagging along. You want to be on your own. Who doesn't?

By now you know how to cross streets safely and how to follow the rules of the road for your bicycle. You probably always buckle your seat belt when you ride in a car and shy away from stray dogs. You watch out for yourself. However, if you really want to take full charge, you need to know how to protect yourself from dangerous strangers.

Most strangers are good people. This book is about the few strangers out there you will want to stay away from or get away from. It's the weirdo, the rare bird you don't want to have anything to do with that you are going to learn about.

Strangers who could mean trouble are not grisly monsters or dirty bums who sleep in the park. Because they almost always seem very normal, you can't recognize strangers who are trying to trap you simply by the way they look. But, you can tell a lot from what is said and how those strangers act.

Every chapter in this book will teach you something new about spotting a stranger who may not be safe. You will learn how to avoid a stranger who might hurt you and how to handle a stranger who tries to trick you. In each story the girl or boy made a choice, but you will read about other choices that are just as good. You may have suggestions of your own. Ask your parents for their ideas and be sure to talk over anything you don't understand with them.

The "You Should Know" and "Always Remember" sections are very important. They contain the facts: how to figure out who is a stranger; safety rules you should never break; risks you should never take; how dangerous strangers operate; how and where to get help. Yes, sometimes you can and should say "No" to a grown-up, disobey an adult's orders or be out and out disrespectful. That's not always so easy, but you'll learn.

The more you know about dangerous strangers the more you can trust yourself if you get into a bind. You will have emergency plans—just like what to do in case of a fire—stored in your head should you ever need them. In no time, your guard will be up and protecting yourself will be easy.

By the time you finish this book your thinking will be so sharp, you will always be able to make good decisions about your own safety. Once you understand what to watch for and how to act, no nasty stranger should be able to outwit you . . . ever.

CHAPTER 1
No Thanks, Stranger

"Can I play?" Hillary asked her mother.

"If your homework is finished," her mom replied.

"It is. I'm going over to Michele's," Hillary answered as she closed the front door.

Hillary was so glad that Michele and her family had bought the house across the street. She and Michele had become very best friends in no time at all. They talked on the telephone every night and tried to see each other every day after school.

"Hi, Michele, can you play?"

"No. Daddy is coming home early tonight for dinner. Mom said I could sit out front for a few minutes."

Hillary and Michele talked about the spelling test they had that day and laughed about the costumes everyone had worn to the school party. They were having the best time when Michele's mother called her back into the house.

"Sorry, Hillary. Really wish I could play. Maybe tomorrow."

"That's okay," Hillary said gloomily as she waved to her friend, "I guess I'll take a little walk until dinner time."

Since Michele had moved in, Hillary did not like to do anything by herself. Even short walks were more fun with Michele. She began thinking about how they could dress up for next year's costume party. Maybe she and Michele could go as twins or monsters from another planet.

Before she knew it, Hillary had walked off her own street. She forgot her mother's warning: never to leave their street without permission.

When she turned around to start back home, she saw a man in a car parked next to the curb. He waved and called her over to the car. "Hi. What's your name?"

"Hillary."

"How would you like an ice cream cone, Hillary?" he asked.

She stopped to think about his offer. He looks like a very nice man. I know I'm not allowed to talk to strangers, but this one is different. He's so friendly.

Hillary was hungry and a little ice cream sounded like a good idea. A small cone would not ruin her dinner and she still had time before her father came home from work. She had nothing else to do.

"Okay," she said to the stranger, "I'd love one." Hillary climbed in and off they drove to the man's house. "I'll have my ice cream and run right home in time for dinner."

They drove and drove. The man lived much farther away than Hillary had thought. "I won't remember how to get home," she said.

"Don't worry, I'll drive you," he told her. "You won't get lost that way."

"I don't know. I guess that will be fine," she answered, but she wasn't really sure.

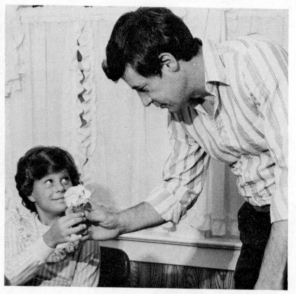

"Here we are. That wasn't so far, was it? It just seems like a long way when you don't know where you're going." The man unlocked his front door, then locked it from the inside.

He took off his sweater and went to the kitchen to make Hillary's cone.

"Fudge twirl," he said. "Hope you like it."

"I better eat this on the way home. It's getting late and I have to set the table. I'm teaching my brother and sister, but they still don't get the fork and spoon in the right places."

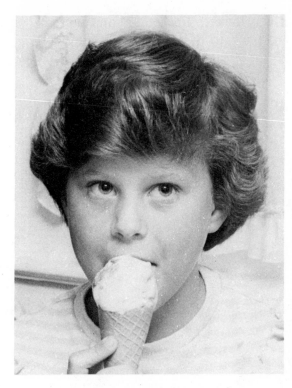

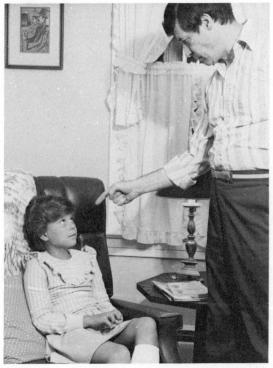

"Finish it here, then I'll take you home."

Hillary did what she was told, but when she finished, the man led her into another room and shouted at her, "I'm not ready to let you go. You're staying here with me until I say you can go home."

"But I don't want to stay here," Hillary told the man. "I want to go home to my mother and daddy and my own room."

"You'll stay with me!"

Hillary begged and begged, "Please let me go, please."

She ran to the door, but it was locked. She pulled and pulled and finally gave up. She went back to the chair. Now she was crying.

At home Hillary's mother was frantic. It was late and Hillary could not be found. She called Michele's house and Michele's mother told Mrs. Grayson, Hillary's mother, that Hillary had not been there for hours. Mrs. Grayson called the neighbors, but no one had seen Hillary.

"We must call the police. They'll help us find Hillary," she said to Hillary's sister. Mrs. Grayson told the police exactly what Hillary looked like, what she was wearing and where she was last seen. "Please find her," she said as she hung up. "Don't worry, Julie, we'll find your sister."

A few minutes later Hillary's father came home. Her brother Gregory ran to meet him. "Daddy, Hillary is missing. We can't find her. She disappeared! Mom called everywhere. We drove around the whole neighborhood looking for her."

Mr. Grayson got back in his car and searched the neighborhood. Mrs. Grayson stayed close to the phone. Julie watched out the window while Gregory sat on the front steps hoping Hillary would come running down the street. They knew she was in trouble.

While Hillary's family waited for some word about her and while Mr. Grayson, the neighbors and the police hunted, Hillary was getting more frightened.

Why won't this man let me go? she wondered. She wanted to be with her mother and father and Gregory and Julie. She asked again, "Can I go home now?"

As he left the room, the man warned her, "No. You sit in that chair and don't move!"

Hillary saw a telephone in the corner on a table. She dashed to it and dialed "O" for operator. "Help, help," she said beginning to cry again. "This man won't let me go home."

"Who is this?" the operator asked.

"It's Hillary," she answered.

"Hillary who? What's your last name?"

"Hillary Grayson."

"Where are you?"

"I don't know."

"What's the phone number?" the operator asked.

"I don't know," Hillary said through her tears.

"Look on the telephone, Hillary."

"Oh, here it is: 999–9987. Please tell my daddy." She heard the man's footsteps and quickly ran back to the chair.

The operator called the police.

The sergeant on duty looked up 999–9987 in his special book that lists the address for any telephone number. He radioed all police cars.

As the message came over the police radio, Officer Moore listened carefully. "This is car 46. I'm at Grove and Elmcrest. Going to 201 Lenox."

Here's 201, he said to himself as he pulled up. The house looked dark—as if no one were home—but he noticed the car parked in front of his.

The policeman walked up the front steps and rang the bell. There was no response. He rang again.

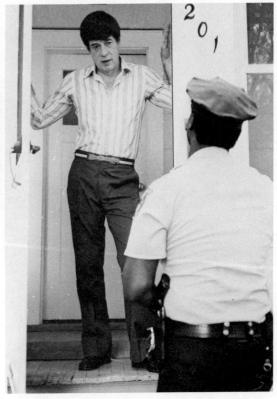

"Yes, officer, can I help you?"

"I'm looking for a little girl named Hillary Grayson. I was told she was here with you."

"No, sir. No Hillary here. Just me," the man replied.

"You sure?"

Before the man could answer, Officer Moore heard a banging sound. "What's that?" He looked in the direction of the noise.

Hillary was pounding on the window and yelling "Help," but Officer Moore could not hear the words.

"Hillary?" he shouted so she could hear him.

"Yes, it's me. Here I am! Here I am!"

"Wait right there. Everything's okay. I'll come in for you in a minute. Don't worry," Officer Moore kept talking to Hillary while he handcuffed the mean man.

He locked the stranger in the police car and radioed for help.

"You know, Hillary, we are lucky to find you. We've been looking for this man for a very long time. He has been locking up little girls in his house and frightening them. You were very smart to remember to use the telephone."

"Thank you," Hillary smiled.

She watched the policeman from car 45 take the mean stranger away. Officer Moore called to the other officer, "Thanks, John. See you back at the station."

Hillary sat very close to Officer Moore and listened carefully to what he was saying. "Now you know why children should not wander off without telling their mothers where they are going. It's not safe to talk to strangers even if they are offering you candy and ice cream or dolls or rides or anything. Right?"

"Right!" Hillary was so glad to be going home.

33

Julie and Greg raced down to see their sister and the police car. "Who would have chased us around the house if you didn't come back?" Greg asked his sister.

"And who would have taught us how to set the table?" Julie shouted with joy.

Hillary ran ahead to her mother. "Where did you find her?" Mrs. Grayson asked as she hugged and kissed Hillary.

"It's a long story," said Officer Moore. He explained the special book that gives addresses for telephone numbers to Mr. Grayson and told him how smart Hillary had been to call the operator for help.

The children and Mrs. Grayson were listening to Hillary. "Mommy, I won't ever wander off the street again. You know ice cream doesn't taste good when a nasty person gives it to you.

"Next time I'll say 'No thanks, stranger' and run."

Hillary made many, many dangerous mistakes. From them you should have learned a lot about dealing with strangers. Did you get it all? Let's make sure:

1. You must be very careful around people you do not know. Anyone you have not seen before is a stranger. With strangers, your best bet is to be unfriendly.

2. As Hillary discovered, you can't tell anything from appearances. The stranger who locked up Hillary looked friendly, trustworthy and harmless.

3. Strangers who plan to take you away will try to win you over and make you their friend by offering you something you might want. This is called a lure. This stranger used ice cream to lure Hillary.

A lure can be something you want more than anything else in the world: a new puppy or kitten, a stuffed animal, a tape recorder or video game, ice skates or a bicycle. But you're strong; you know better. You'll say "No." *Don't* accept anything from a stranger, not even a single penny.

4. Never agree to go anywhere with a stranger.

5. You must be especially cautious when you are alone.

6. This man did not force Hillary into the car, but if someone orders you into a car, run as fast as you can to the closest house or store for help. Ask someone to call the police at once.

7. Like Hillary, you are very special. You are an important part of your family. If you disappeared with a stranger, no one would know where to find you. You are not going to let that happen because you have learned from Hillary's experience that nothing a stranger might offer you is worth being separated from the people who love you the most.

1. Tell a parent where you are going *before* you go.

2. If you change your plans or are going to be late, let your parents know. Stop long enough to call them.

3. Don't tell strangers your name, where you live or anything personal about your family and friends.

4. Stand back from cars out of the driver's or passenger's reach. Only take a ride if you know the person very well and have permission from your parents.

5. Don't go into a stranger's house—even with a friend.

6. Don't go into *anyone's* house, and that includes neighbors' and friends' houses, unless you have special permission from your parents. You should not go into the house of the man around the corner or down the block just because your parents are friendly with him. Get a parent's okay first.

7. Call the police, dial the operator or phone home if you are in trouble. Make the call that is quickest and easiest for you.

8. In any situation with a mean stranger, do not panic. Try to remain calm so that you can think about a safe escape or way to get help. Hillary found a phone and used it quickly.

CHAPTER 2
Pick of the Litter

A few blocks from David's house there is a park. David and his friends meet in the park playground almost every afternoon. When David left his house his mother reminded him, "If Christopher and Tom are not there, come right back."

Chris and Tom were not at the playground. David's other friend, Sam, wasn't there either. No one was in the playground, but David decided to take a quick swing ride before going home. He hoped one of his friends would show up soon. He was swinging happily when he saw a man walking toward him.

"Hello, having fun?" the man asked. David looked at the kitten the man was carrying and stopped the swing. He saw this man whenever he visited his father's office, but did not know his name. He's not a real stranger. I know him slightly. It will be okay to talk to him, David thought.

"Can I hold her for a minute?" David reached for the kitten. He loved kittens.

"Sure. Cute, isn't she? Her name is Princess. Do you have a kitten?" the man asked as he handed Princess to David.

"No, I wish I did."

"Here, sit down so you can pet her. She's frisky, so hold on to her. Princess is promised to my neighbors, but if you come home with me you can pick out any kitten you like. There are five of them."

At first that seemed like a great idea. David was excited until he remembered that his mother was not terribly fond of cats. "I don't think my mother would like a kitten."

David listened carefully. "If she doesn't like it, you can give it back to me. Come on, I live on Spruce Street. You know where that is?"

David nodded. "You'll take it back if my mom says I can't keep it?" He really wanted a kitten.

"I promise," the man smiled.

David had a funny feeling about the man even though he sort of knew him. "No, no, I better not go. I have to ask my mother first," he told the man.

David was lucky. The man reached down, took Princess and waved, "Okay, tell me tomorrow."

He sat on the ground until the man was out of sight and then ran home to tell his mother about the man from Dad's office and the kitten.

David's Other Choices

1. David knew that he was not permitted to play alone in the park. He should have left the playground as soon as he realized his friends weren't there.

2. When the man began to talk to him, he could have said "I have to go now, my mother is waiting." (Even if it wasn't true!)

You Should Know

1. A stranger is someone you don't know well. If you don't know someone's name and where he lives, and if he is not a *very* close friend of your parents, he is a stranger.

2. Whenever you see someone you "know a little" in a place you don't usually see him, you should wonder what he is doing there and be extra careful. Don't go with that person and don't take whatever he is offering.

3. To convince you to go off with them, strangers will tempt you with false promises. These promises range from the promise to David of the pick of the litter to a trip to an amusement park, arcade or carnival, to the beach, to a movie or ballgame. Can you think of more? What promises and offers would you find hard to refuse?

4. Well-meaning strangers will not give you gifts without first asking your parents if they may do so.

Always Remember

1. Don't play in deserted parks, empty lots or abandoned buildings. Secluded places such as the woods and open fields are off limits, too. Keep away from railroad tracks, crossings and stations.

2. Don't play alone away from home.

3. Don't take *anything* from a stranger without permission from a parent.

4. Trust your instincts as David did. You'll find they are usually right.

CHAPTER 3
Your Mother Sent Me

School was almost over for the year. Only a few days remained before summer vacation. At three o'clock sharp, the bell rang and the children ran out of the hot classrooms.

Amy was going straight from school to the dentist. She watched her friends leave school and wished she could go home to play, too. She didn't like the dentist very much.

Amy got tired of waiting for her mother and sat down. She knew her mother would be there soon. When Amy realized that she had been waiting quite a while, she began to worry. Her mother was rarely late. She didn't notice the nice-looking lady who had been watching her.

The stranger walked over to Amy, who stood up politely as she had been taught to do. "Hi, honey," the woman said. "Your mother sent me to get you."

"Who are you?" Amy questioned.

"A friend of your mother's. We went to high school together."

"You did? I never met you. Where is my mother?"

"She had to take your grandmother to the hospital. We're supposed to meet your mother at the hospital."

"What's wrong with my grandma?"

The woman didn't answer Amy's question. Instead she said, "I'll tell you on the way."

Amy was very worried about her grandmother. She loved her so much. Her grandmother met her whenever her mother could not. Amy wasn't sure what to do. She had never seen her mother's friend.

"Come on, it's all right," the woman told her.

"I don't know," Amy replied.

"Come on, right now," the pretty lady urged. "Your mother is waiting for us. And your grandmother will want to see you."

Amy wondered why this lady did not say "Hi, your code word is 'grapefruit.'" Then she would have known for sure that her mother really had sent this woman. Amy wanted to go to the hospital, but her mother and father told her never to go with a stranger unless he or she said the code word. And never, never ask for it, her parents had warned. She didn't ask.

Amy left the woman standing with her hand out and ran back into the school to find a teacher or the secretary in the office to talk to the stranger outside.

Amy's Other Choices

1. When the lady did not say the code word right away, Amy should have gone back into the school to tell the principal, a teacher or someone in the office.

2. She could have said "No" in the beginning and told the woman to come inside with her to talk to the principal or other school official.

3. Amy finally did the right thing, but she really waited too long.

You Should Know

1. Most strangers who try to pick up children are men, but sometimes that stranger could be a woman.

2. Most harmful strangers seem very friendly, just like the woman talking to Amy.

3. Your parents would never send a stranger to bring you home from school or to meet you if someone in the family were hurt or in the hospital.

4. Who has permission to meet you and bring you home? Your grandparents? Aunts? Cousins? The babysitter? Friends? Neighbors? Which ones? Find out. If you ride the school bus, make a plan with your parents of what to do if you miss the bus.

5. Adults will lie if they want to trick you. They will say anything to frighten, worry or confuse you: "There's a fire at your house, come with me." "Your father had a heart attack. We must go to the hospital." "Your mother was in a very serious car accident." "Your dog was run over and your mother took him to the vet. She said to bring you there." Got it? All phony emergencies to make you forget you are going with a stranger. Don't believe a word!

6. In a real emergency, you should know what will happen and what you are supposed to do. Go over the steps with your parents so you're prepared—just in case. Will they call the school to alert the principal? Are you to go to a friend's house? Are you to meet them somewhere?

1. Tell your teacher, the principal or someone in the school office if you see a person you have never seen before hanging around outside or inside school. Don't worry if you point out someone who really belongs there. Your parents and teachers will be pleased that you are being watchful and alert.

2. Code words save a lot of worrying and guessing. A code word is a secret word only you and your family know. The person greeting you must say it to you so you know instantly that this is someone your parents sent. (Read more about code words on page 113.)

If you and your parents think code words are too confusing, observe this standard policy: If your parent or other specified person is not there to meet you, return to the school office until a parent calls with instructions.

3. Crafty strangers can show up anywhere, including your driveway or backyard. They arrive on foot as well as by car. Pay attention to what's going on around you even when you are near your own house.

4. If a stranger talks to you through your backyard fence, comes through your gate or stands in your driveway, run into your house immediately and tell your parent or the person who is taking care of you.

CHAPTER 4

Which Way to the Police Station?

Eric and his friend Matt do everything together. One day Matt was sick and Eric walked home from school alone. He followed the route his mother had picked because it was the safest. He walked past lots of stores, and the streets were usually crowded with people until the last few blocks.

He was a short distance from home when a man shouted to him, "I'm lost. How do I get to the police station?"

"Let's see," Eric began, "this is 8th Street. Go up to that corner and turn right . . ." He was standing away from the car in the middle of the street.

"Wait. I can't hear you. Could you come closer? Now what did you say?"

Eric leaned on the car and started again. "Go to the corner and turn right, like I said. Then go left on Walker Boulevard. That's about two streets up. You'll see the station. It's opposite a big drugstore."

"Let me see if I have it straight." Eric listened as the man repeated his directions. "Up at this corner I go right. Follow that street until I hit Walker, then turn right again."

"No, no," Eric said, "go . . ."

"Why don't you get in and show me. It will only take me a minute in the police station. Just have to drop off some papers. You can come in with me, then I'll buy you a soda and drive you home. Get your bag."

That's when Eric started to think. "No," he laughed, but he
was scared. "Mister, you can't miss the police station," he said
and backed away from the car quickly.

"Get back here," the stranger ordered. "Come back and get
in this car. You listen to me," he yelled. "Get in this car now!"

Eric was long gone. He ran and didn't stop until he reached
his front door.

Eric's Other Choices

1. He could have shouted "I don't know" from across the street and run away.

2. He could have shouted the directions from across the street.

3. He could have not answered and kept walking.

All of these are much safer choices.

You Should Know

1. People who are truly lost ask adults, not children, for directions. There's a big difference between a grown-up asking for help and your asking a grown-up for help. When you ask for help you choose the person and that's very important. Don't let a stranger pick you out.

2. "Where's the police station?" is a very clever question. The police station is a safe place and most of us would think: If someone is asking for the police station he must be okay. Wrong. That question was meant to throw Eric off guard.

When a stranger asks you how to find the hospital, the library, the nursery school, fire department, post office or other place you consider very safe, stay back. The question may be an underhanded trick.

3. Honorable strangers do not invite or order children into their cars.

4. Evil-minded adults will automatically try to take advantage because they think children are taught to obey grown-ups at all times. This stranger thought Eric would hop in the car when he commanded him to do so. Don't listen to or follow a stranger's orders.

5. Had Eric's friend Matt been with him, the stranger probably would not have stopped. Unkind strangers usually approach children who are alone. Buddy-up all the time.

6. Travel the safest route wherever you go. Go over your routes with your parents to be sure there are safe places to stop if you need them. Do not take shortcuts and don't linger along the way.

7. Strangers looking for children drive vans, cars, jeeps and trucks. Old ones, new ones, fancy ones, beat-up ones. Don't get fooled by a shiny new car. Be extra cautious around vans.

Always Remember
___

1. Stand back—out of reach, ready to run—if any vehicle stops or pulls up to ask you a question. Eric stood much too close to the driver.

2. It's safest to shout "I don't know" and walk away or run toward people.

3. Run in the direction the car is *not* going, so the driver will have a hard time following you, but make sure the way is clear. Look over your options to see that nothing or no one is blocking the path you choose.

4. If you can do so safely, try to get a description of the car and driver. Jot down the license plate number in the dirt, in a notebook or in the dust of a parked car. Tell an adult to call the police immediately.

5. Do not believe a stranger who tells you something "will only take a minute," "we'll be right back" or a similar tale.

6. Never ride anywhere with someone you don't know. Do not sit in a stranger's car to get out of the rain or snow while you wait for someone.

CHAPTER 5
A Doll for Jessica

"See, Mommy, this one. This is the one I want. Isn't she beautiful?" Jessica had convinced her mother to look at the toys in Fletcher-Green's Department Store.

"We'll see," answered Mrs. Burke. "Now let's go buy your brother's pajamas."

"Please. Let me look at the dolls."

"Okay, but you wait right here. I'm going over there. See the sign that says BOYS? I'll be back in a few minutes."

Jessica took down another doll. She was trying to figure out how she could convince her mother to buy her one. Her Aunt Jane had just given her a bride doll for her birthday. She knew her mother would not buy her another one so soon. She just knew it.

Oh well, it's fun looking at them and pretending. She was talking to one of the dolls when a stranger knelt next to her.

"Hi, what's your name?" the man asked.

"Hi. You surprised me. My name's Jessica."

"That's a very pretty doll. Does she have a name?"

"No, but I would call her Cindy if she were mine."

"Would you like that doll?" the stranger asked.

"Oh, yes," Jessica told the man, "but I don't think my mother will buy her for me. She said 'We'll see.' Everybody knows what that means."

"How about I buy it for you?" the stranger suggested.

"I don't think my mother would like that. I don't know. It doesn't seem right."

"Your mother won't mind."

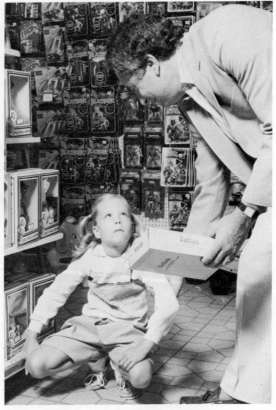

"Yes she will. You don't know her."

"Your mom will be very happy, Jessica. Just think, she won't have to buy it and you won't be pestering her to buy it for you. Come on." The man took the doll from Jessica and helped her up.

"No, my mom told me to wait here. I'm staying right here."

The man took Jessica's arm and smiled at her. "That's okay. We'll pay for the doll and come back. It will only take a minute. We can pay for Cindy down at the end of the aisle. See there." He pointed to the checkout desk.

"No," Jessica answered, "I'll stay here."

He was holding her very tightly and she could not get away. "Let's go," he said in a mean voice.

When he started to pull Jessica, she began to yell. "Let go. Let go. You don't know me. You're not my father. Help."

The man pulled harder. Jessica yelled as loudly as she could over and over, "Let go. You don't know me. Help. This man is kidnapping me."

The man let go and ran down the aisle.

Jessica stood there. She was afraid to move and she was too frightened to cry. People came running from every direction, but Mrs. Burke heard Jessica's first plea for help and got to her before anyone else.

Jessica ran into her mother's arms. Mrs. Burke held her daughter tightly.

"I'm very proud of you, Jessica. People could hear you yelling all over the store. You shouted just the right thing. You scared that horrible man away."

Jessica's Other Choices

1. Jessica should have walked to the Boys Department to find her mother as soon as the man started talking to her.

2. If she had been able to pull away from the man, she could have run to the Boys Department or to the first employee or shopper she saw. (Only go to your parent if you know exactly where he or she is.) When Jessica realized the man was not going to let go, she took the very best action.

You Should Know

1. A total stranger who had good intentions would not come up to you in a store and offer to buy you something.

2. A dangerous stranger can look and act as pleasant as your mother or father. He or she can be dressed in a business suit, sports clothes or in a police or firefighter's uniform. This type of stranger can be very neat or not so well put together.

3. If someone grabs you and there is no one close by, make up a story to help you get away or do all those nasty things you are usually not permitted to do—bite, kick, scratch—*if you think you can do so safely*.

If someone is mean enough to hold you by force, then you have every right to fight. Hit hard. Go for his shins, eyes, knees with all your might. A powerful surprise attack may shock him into letting go. Then run for help.

4. Yelling and struggling attract attention. Pull things off shelves; crash bottles to the floor. Make a mess and make a big fuss.

Mean strangers do not like such scenes. They hope you will go with them quietly. If you yell loud and long, there is a very good chance that the stranger will release you.

5. When you yell, shout things such as "You don't know me!" "I'm being kidnapped!" "You're not my father!" so people will realize that you are not having a fight with your parent. You want everyone around to know that you are not having a temper tantrum either, that a stranger is trying to take you against your will.

6. Yelling is not the same as raising your voice in an angry fight. Yelling is strong and powerful. A yell comes from deep down, from your lungs and stomach, not from your throat. Yelling means business. Practice yelling using Jessica's words.

7. When you yell for help in crowded areas or stores, single out the person you want by describing her: "Lady with the baby, stop this man." "Lady in the red dress, this is not my father. Help me." "Lady in the blue coat, this man is taking me away. I don't know him." Call to different people until one of them comes to your rescue.

Always Remember

1. If someone grabs, you *yell*. Calling for help is not a babyish thing to do. It's very smart. Do it.

2. Do not allow any guard or officially dressed person to force you from the spot where your parent told you to wait. If he does that, he is probably a phony. Yell to a shopper to come over and help you. Do *not* go. Wait for your parent to return and straighten out the problem. Speak up and talk back if you have to.

3. Jessica knew where her mother was. But, if you are separated from your parent in a large department store, shopping center or grocery store, do not search. Go to the nearest clerk or checkout counter for help. The store will use a loudspeaker to call your mother or father. *Never, ever go to the parking lot.* And, *Do not go home alone,* even if you live close by.

4. Do not sit alone in a car—even with the doors locked—while one of your parents runs an errand. Insist that you go along. Tell your parents that you do not like being left in the car and that the car is a very dangerous place to wait.

CHAPTER 6

Ralph, the Lost Puppy

Soccer was Michael's favorite sport. He was good at it. On his way to soccer practice one day, he dribbled, gave the ball a boot, then dribbled some more.

He dribbled the ball carefully to keep it on the sidewalk. He didn't like chasing the ball into the street.

He missed a dribble and ran up to stop the fast-rolling ball. "Hey, that's mine," Michael shouted when he saw a man get to the ball before he did.

"I know, son. Here it is. Just trying to help."
"Thanks, sir. Thanks a lot," Michael smiled.
"Where you off to?" the man asked.
"Soccer practice."

"Can you help me out? I lost my new puppy. Will you help me look for him?" the man questioned, waving an empty leash.
"Sorry, sir. Can't. Practice starts in five minutes."
"We'll find him in no time. He has to be right here, somewhere in these trees. Little fellow just slipped right out of his leash when I ran over to stop your ball from rolling into the street."
"Sorry," Michael repeated, "have to go."

"But he's so tiny. Only ten weeks old. He's just a baby. He'll be hungry soon."

Michael felt sorry for the man and was worried about the puppy. He felt it was his fault that the puppy had slipped away. He wanted to search, but he knew if he did he would be late for practice. Late meant being benched. The coach was strict about tardiness.

The man pretended he did not hear Michael, he kept talking. "When we find Ralph—that's the puppy's name—I'll take some pictures of you and Ralph to show your parents. They'll be real proud of you for finding a lost dog."

Michael paid close attention to what the man was saying, but he didn't like the way the stranger kept moving closer and closer to him. He was friendly enough. He reminded Michael of his music instructor, but this man was too pushy. He kept trying to convince Michael to search for Ralph.

"We'll start across the street." The man pointed with one hand and put the other one on Michael's shoulder. "Listen," he added, "I'll give you five dollars. A reward for helping me find Ralph. I'll pay you whether or not we find him. How's that for a good deal?"

"Don't touch me." Michael backed off. He didn't like being touched by someone he didn't know. He thought for a split second: home or the field?

The field. It's closer and this time of day the field is safe. His
teammates would be at the bench and Coach Henry would be
waiting. Michael ran away from the stranger.

He ran fast. He ran onto the field.

Without stopping, he checked to see if the man was chasing him. He ran as fast as he could, clutching his soccer ball.

He ran until he reached Coach Henry on the far side of the field.

Michael's Other Choices

1. He could have thanked the man, taken his ball and immediately run to the field. Don't take chances with strangers. Be impolite if necessary.

2. He could have kept way out of the stranger's reach while they talked.

You Should Know

1. Strangers who continue to try to convince you to help them after you have said "No" can be dangerous. Do not get involved in what they are saying. You do not have to be helpful. Leave.

2. Strangers who want to take your picture probably are up to no good. Run away.

3. Strangers who promise you money are definite trouble. If a stranger waves money at you, don't be a wise guy. Don't think you might be lucky enough to grab it and get away before he grabs you. Don't try!

4. Only a harmful stranger would try to make you feel guilty. This man tried to make Michael feel responsible for the dog's disappearance. Besides, we don't know for sure that a dog named Ralph really existed, do we?

Always Remember

1. A stranger who continues to move toward you after you have refused his request or after you have backed away to show that you are afraid is not respecting your feelings. This is someone you do not want to be near.

2. Tell your parents if anyone wants to take your picture or promises to make you a movie star. An honest stranger who wanted to do any of these things would discuss it with your parents before mentioning it to you.

3. Any time a grown-up attempts to pressure you or force you into something you don't want to do, report the whole story to an adult you trust.

4. Should you ever have to get away from a stranger, as Michael had to do, drop your toys, jacket, ball, even your bike. The most important thing is to get away. You can return with an adult later to pick up what you left behind. If they're gone, just remember that your possessions can be replaced—you can't.

CHAPTER 7
A Quick Ride

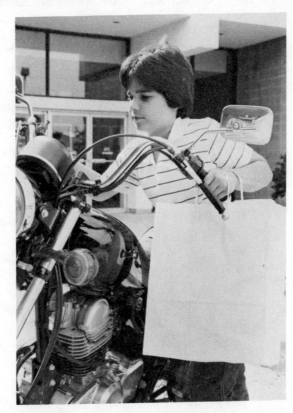

Todd saw the parked motorcycle the second he came out of the mall.

His Uncle Bill had a cycle, but Todd's parents did not let him ride with his uncle no matter how much Todd begged. He put down his shopping bags to get a closer look.

He checked the dials on the dashboard, looked over the motor and decided this was much better and probably faster than his Uncle Bill's cycle.

"Hi, I'm Kirk. What's your name?" the owner of the motor-cycle asked.

"Todd."

"Like my bike?" Kirk asked. "It's brand new. See, not a hundred miles on it yet. Want a ride?"

"Do I? Are you kidding?" Todd loved the idea, but his father had told him to wait right at the mall entrance. "I can't. Thanks anyway. I'm not allowed on motorcycles and my dad will be out in a minute."

Kirk walked around and put the key in the ignition. "A quick one. Just around the parking lot. Your dad won't know. He probably wouldn't care if you stayed away for a few days," said Kirk, trying to find out if Todd had had a fight with his father or was unhappy at home.

"Come on, Todd, aren't you my friend? We'll have fun!"

While Kirk got on his motorcycle and unhooked the spare helmet, Todd was remembering how angry his father had been yesterday when Todd showed him his report card. "If you don't do better," he had yelled, "there's going to be real trouble." Maybe my Dad doesn't want me. I'm such a bad student, Todd thought.

"Here, put on this helmet."

"Okay," Todd agreed, "but only for a short ride here in the parking lot."

"We're going to have a great time. You'll see," Kirk promised. "Hop on back."

"I don't know. My father is going to be really mad if I go for a ride. He doesn't let me go on my uncle's motorcycle. I'm in enough trouble because of my report card. I better not."

Todd took off the extra helmet and gave it back. "But I thought we were friends. Don't you trust me?" Kirk asked, hoping Todd would change his mind.

"Sure, sure, I trust you," he said, but didn't really mean it. "I can't go." Todd picked up his packages. "Thanks anyway, Kirk. Maybe another time."

Todd's Other Choices

1. He could have waited at the shopping mall entrance as he had been told to do.

2. He could have moved away from the motorcycle the minute its owner appeared.

3. He could not have talked to the stranger, and could have gone back into the mall and stood next to or near an adult or group of people.

4. If Kirk had followed him inside the mall, Todd could have gone to any adult for help.

You Should Know

1. Strangers look for children by themselves at shopping centers, fairgrounds, sporting events, carnivals and campsites. Stick close to your parents or friends in those places.

2. If you must meet or wait for someone at a shopping center, arrange to do so at the busiest entrances, not at infrequently used ones like those near rear parking lots and service areas.

3. A stranger who wants to take you somewhere may try to convince you that he is your friend. How could he be your friend? He just met you!

4. The strangers you want to avoid may try to tell you that your parents don't really want you. Even if you've just been fighting with your parents, you know that's *not true*.

Always Remember

1. It's a bad idea to talk to strangers.

2. Do not consider taking even a quick ride with a stranger.

3. A dangerous stranger can be young or old. He can be a teenager from your own or a nearby neighborhood.

4. Should you find that you have slipped into a conversation with a stranger, speak clearly and confidently. Don't mumble or shuffle your feet and don't use words like "maybe," "I don't know," or "I suppose." Act sure of yourself.

You want any stranger—good or bad—to think that you are capable of taking care of yourself and that you have a mind of your own. This type of behavior tells a stranger that he or she cannot push you around or take advantage of you.

5. Be cautious around someone you don't know who says he is your friend.

6. Get away from anyone who tells you that you will have more fun with him, that your parents don't love you. How would he know?

CHAPTER 8
Jennifer Home Alone

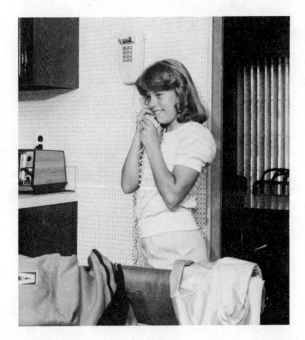

The first thing Jennifer does every day when she comes home from school is call her mother at work. "Hi, Mom. It's Jen. Guess what? I got an A on the History test."

"That's great, Jennifer. You'll be on the honor roll again. We like that. Did you lock the door?"

"Yes, I did."

"Don't forget to have something to eat," her mother told her. All day in school she had been thinking about the cookies she and her mother had baked on Sunday.

"Don't worry, I'll have a snack," she laughed. "The cookies, remember? Suzi said she was coming over later. I'm going to do my homework first. See you after work. . . . Okay, I won't forget. I'll set the table for dinner. Love you. 'Bye."

Jennifer poured herself a glass of milk, piled peanut chocolate chip cookies on a plate and emptied her bookbag. She did math first because that was her favorite subject. She was studying English when the telephone rang.

"Hi, Suzi. Finished math. Just started studying for the English test. It'll be easy, don't you think? . . . Bring your English book so we can quiz each other. Okay?"

Jennifer munched a cookie while Suzi chatted about what they could buy Heather for her birthday. Their friend's party was next week and they were combining their money to buy Heather a joint present. "We could get her tapes. I don't think she has . . ."

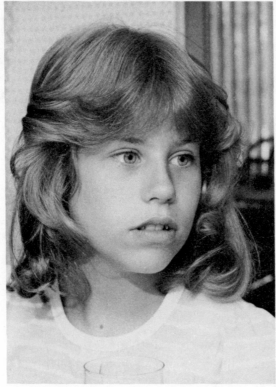

"Have to go, Suzi. There's someone at the door. I'll stop English and work on Science until you get here."

Jennifer hung up the phone. Who can that be? she wondered. Mother didn't tell me anyone was coming.

The bell rang again. "I'm coming," Jennifer shouted. She looked out the window and saw a man she didn't know.

"Hi. My car is stuck out front. Flat tire. My wife is very sick and I have to get home." The smiling man seemed harmless. Jennifer wanted to ask him what was wrong with his wife, but she didn't.

"Can I use your telephone to call a garage?"

"No," Jennifer answered loudly through the window. "I'm not allowed to let strangers in the house. Do you want me to call a garage for you?"

"Where's your mother?" the man smiled.

"She's busy," Jennifer lied.

"Go ask her."

"No, I can't do that. You better go next door," Jennifer suggested.

"Please, let me use your phone." He made his fist into a telephone receiver to be sure Jennifer understood. "I must get home to my wife."

"No, sorry. Go next door."

"You're not being nice," the man told Jennifer.

"You can't come in," Jennifer told him boldly. She stuck to her guns and repeated, "Go next door."

The man backed away from the door. Jennifer waited until he reached his car, then ran to the phone to call her next-door neighbors and her mother.

Jennifer's Other Choices

1. She could not have answered the door at all. You and your parents should decide whether or not they want you to pretend no one is home. They may prefer that you go to the door and follow their specific instructions.

2. She could have called a neighbor right away.

3. She could have called the police.

You Should Know

1. Dangerous people who ring doorbells have many excuses: They pretend to be repairmen; they pretend there is an emergency; they try to make a delivery of groceries, flowers, appliances, dry cleaning; they tell you they are your parents' dear old friends.

2. If a delivery person says you must sign for the package, tell him to take it to a neighbor's house or to come back later. Don't open the door!

3. Ask a parent to arrange a "backup" neighbor, one who is usually home when you are, so that you can call that person if you have a problem you can't handle. Call this neighbor whenever an adult you don't know rings your doorbell.

4. Whatever excuse a stranger uses, don't fall for it. If they need the telephone, offer to place the call. You are helping without putting yourself in danger.

Always Remember

1. Wearing your key around your neck is a sure sign that you go into your house alone. Hide your key in a pocket, knapsack, bookbag or under your clothing.

2. Lock the door after you let yourself in.

3. Don't tell anyone at the door or on the telephone that you are home alone. Make up a "white lie" just as Jennifer did. Saying "My mom (or dad) is busy" is all you need to say to a stranger. Don't explain and don't answer further questions.

4. You may open the door for close relatives, but for no one else without a special go-ahead from a parent. Don't open the door for the police unless you have called them. Call your mom or dad at work if people at the door insist they should be allowed into the house.

5. If you go out without calling a parent at work, leave a note that says where you have gone and when you will return.

CHAPTER 9
Help Me, Please

Brian was annoyed. His friends were late again. They were always late. He thought about leaving and wondered if they would hang around waiting for him. He didn't think so, but he decided to give them five more minutes.

A man who had bought a few things at the supermarket was pushing his cart out toward his parked car. He was looking for a young boy to help him put his groceries into the car.

He saw Brian leaning against a pole by himself. He adjusted the sling on his arm and approached Brian.

"Hi. I'm Mr. Perry. Can you give me a hand with these bags?"

"I don't know. I'm waiting for my friends," Brian answered.

"My car's right over here. I can't lift heavy bundles with this arm."

Brian had a hard decision to make. He felt sorry for the man, but he also knew he was not supposed to talk to strangers. "Okay, sure thing. I'll help. Where's your car?"

The man opened the trunk and struggled with a grocery bag until Brian took it from him. "Come around to this side," Mr. Perry said, "it'll be easier."

"That's it. Fine. You sure are a good-looking fellow," Mr. Perry smiled. Brian blushed. "It's very nice of you to help me. I appreciate it. This bad arm is a real pain. Know what I mean?"

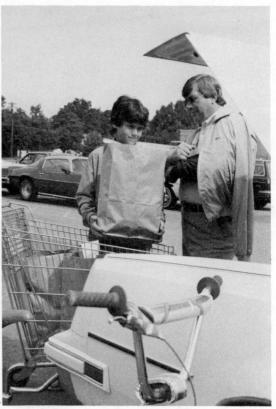

Brian was about to lean in front of the man to put the bag in the trunk when he saw out of the corner of his eye that this stranger was faking. Mr. Perry was starting to remove the sling.

This man is going to grab me, Brian thought. That's why he wanted me to come around to the other side of the shopping cart.

Brian didn't hesitate one second. He dropped the grocery bag and raced off on his bike as fast as his legs would pedal.

Brian's Other Choices

1. Brian could have said "Sorry, no. I can't help you."
2. He could have ignored Mr. Perry's request for help and pedaled away immediately.

You Should Know

1. Strangers who want to take you somewhere with them are very good at pretending they can't do something themselves and need your help. They may even try to make you feel sorry for them.
2. Pretending strangers can be anywhere: outside a library, outside a department store, in front of their own houses or in front of your house. They might say they need help carrying books, moving crates, climbing a ladder, planting a bush, spread-

ing gravel or dirt. The lies they make up to get your assistance are endless.

3. To attract your attention, these sneaky strangers may walk with canes or crutches. Some, like Mr. Perry, will wear a sling that they don't need. Others, who really are young, will dress up to look like old ladies or men.

4. It is very difficult to figure out who is trying to fool you and who really needs help. If you are like most kids, you will want to help. If you think the person truly needs a hand, be on the alert. Watch carefully as Brian did.

5. It's not smart to hang around parking lots.

6. Watch out for strangers who flatter you by saying things such as "You're cute," "You're good-looking," "You're smart," "You do that very well" (whatever you happen to be doing at the moment). They're trying to be friendly—too friendly.

Always Remember

1. Be on guard if you ever encounter a stranger who asks for help. Be especially suspicious if giving help involves going into or near the person's car, van or house.

2. It is perfectly fine to ignore or say "No" to an adult you don't know. Don't feel bad because you did not help a stranger. You are protecting yourself. That's the most important thing you have to do. Don't forget it.

3. Use your own good judgment. Trust your instincts. If the situation looks fishy, avoid it.

4. If you do decide to help out, stand clear of the stranger— far enough away so that he cannot grab you or force you into his car.

CHAPTER 10
Smart Move

Kate hardly ever went shopping by herself, but this was a special occasion. It was her mother's birthday. She picked out a sweater that she knew her mother would love. Kate had saved and saved to be able to buy it without asking her father for money.

On her way home she stopped to look in the window of her favorite store. She checked the whole window before she found the bear she wanted. She was figuring out how many weeks' allowance she would need when she had an odd feeling that someone was watching her.

At first she didn't move, but she could see that the man had moved closer. She wasn't sure what she should do. She decided that the man must be window shopping too.

    She started away from the store slowly, then turned to see what the man was doing. There he was, right behind her.

    She walked a little farther and stopped. This time Kate took a longer look and began to walk faster. I wonder what that man wants? she asked herself.

Is he following me? Kate began to worry. Maybe I'm imagining this. She talked to herself. You're crazy, she told herself. She moved toward the middle of the sidewalk and headed for the corner to cross the street.

She made one more fast check. The man was closer. Too close. He's following me! Kate was scared. She started over to the woman on the bench. She would point out the man and ask the lady what she should do.

Then she remembered the pet store was coming up. She and her mother had stopped in many times to look at the puppies and to buy fish food. She felt better about asking for help in there. She raced to it, stepped in, then back to get one last look at the man.

She told the clerk in the pet store that she thought a man was following her. Kate described the man: "He's very tall with brown hair and wearing a tan suit. He's older than my father." The salesclerk called the police and Kate's mother, who came to take her home.

Kate's Other Choices

1. She could have run over to the woman sitting on the bench or walked toward a group of people.

2. She could have stopped another adult in the street and asked for help.

3. If the man had come any closer, Kate could have yelled as loudly as she could for help and run as fast as she could into any shop.

You Should Know

1. If you think someone is following you, don't wait until you are sure. Tell someone right away.

2. Walk toward people and crowds. Do not try to get away from a stranger by running down alleys or quiet side streets. Stay in the middle of the sidewalk, not close to the doorways of buildings.

3. Most adults will help you if you ask them to.

4. Police officers and women with children are the safest people to ask for help, but if you need help fast, choose the person who is closest to you.

5. You can give the police valuable information by remembering how the person looked: Was he tall or short? Fat or skinny? Did he have brown, gray, black or blond hair? A mustache? Was he wearing a yellow sweater, a dark blue suit or a short-sleeve striped shirt? Was his tie red? Did he wear a hat? Glasses? Anything you remember will help the police find that person.

6. If you think you are being followed and you are near your house, run home. If you know no one is home, run to your closest neighbor's or friend's house. Go to *any* house for protection if you are in a strange neighborhood and you believe someone is trying to catch up with you.

Always Remember

1. Don't be embarrassed to get help—anywhere, anytime. If someone is bothering you on the street, in a store, in the subway or on a bus, tell an adult what is happening.

2. Do not try to hide. You could get trapped and not be able to run.

3. If you think you are being followed on a bus or the subway, tell the bus driver, train conductor or subway police. Do not get off until you have found help.

4. If you think someone has followed you home, do not go into your apartment or house alone. Find a neighbor to go in with you or go to a friend's house.

CHAPTER 11
Getting Smarter

You're well on your way to understanding everything about safety with strangers. There are still some things you must be sure to remember before you are completely "stranger-wise." You always want to know, not guess, what to do, what to say or where to call.

Where do you live? In the Northeast? Midwest? South? Look at a map. Do you know your full name and address, including city and state? You will need this information if you are lost or forget your telephone number.

Telephone Basics

Do you know your telephone number and area code? You *must* be able to call home from anywhere. That's why your area code is very important. It carries your phone call to the right part of your state if you are calling from far away.

Here are some long-distance tips: You can usually talk to an operator without money on a pay telephone. If you forget your area code, call the operator by dialing or pressing "O" on any telephone. Tell her what city and state you live in. She will give you your area code and dial the number for you if you tell her it's an emergency.

If you forget your telephone number, tell the operator your name, your parents' names and where you live. She will find the number, but you must explain why you want her to make the call.

Be sure you learn: how to dial long distance; how to use a pay telephone; how to reach your parents at work.

Do you know both parents' first names? Is one of your parents' last names different from yours? What is it?

Do you know the telephone numbers of people you might need if you cannot find your parents or if the line is busy? Do you know a neighbor's number? Your mother's best friend's or your grandmother's telephone number?

Be prepared. Is there a list of important telephone numbers posted near one of the telephones in your house? Be sure the police emergency number is on it. That's one number you should memorize.

Carry a piece of paper with all your emergency phone numbers if you cannot remember them. Tape coins to a notebook or always carry emergency phone money in your pocket or purse.

Police Are Your Friends

Police officers are trained to protect you. They care about you and want you to feel safe. Many are parents like your mother and father. If you are in trouble, the police can and will help you.

Calling the police. From most public phones you need no money to reach the police emergency line. The operator can also dial the police for you. When you call, be ready to supply the information needed to help you quickly. Speak clearly and loudly. Tell the police:

1. Your name and where you live.
2. Where you are, unless you don't know.
3. Exactly what the problem is.
4. The number on the telephone you are using.

Call the police or find a police officer immediately if:
—Someone has taken you somewhere you do not want to be.
—Someone is threatening you.
—Someone is following you and there is no one to tell and no place to run for safety.
—You feel you are in trouble and have only a few seconds to make a call for help.
—You are lost or hurt and cannot find an adult.

In Public

Ballfields, sports arenas, amusement and community parks, playgrounds, fairs and carnivals are great fun, but they are also perfect places for a mean stranger to tempt you and win you over.

When you're out having a good time playing or shopping:
—Stay with your family or friends. Don't wander off by yourself.
—If you do find yourself alone and in need of assistance, ask people who work there such as vendors or security guards.
—Have a plan in case one of the members of your group gets lost. That can happen quite easily in busy places such as fairs

and shopping malls. Pick a meeting place first thing when you arrive at your destination.

—If you forget to choose a meeting place and are lost in a shopping center or mall, wait near the spot you last saw your parent. If she does not find you, go into a store and ask an employee behind a counter to help you.

—Do not accept help from someone who comes up to you. Remember, *you* do the picking. It's safer that way.

—*Never* permit a stranger to take you home. If your parent does not show up, ask a store manager or someone in the store's offices to call the police for you.

Go away, mister. Pretend you are at a carnival and your parents allowed you to stay and play a certain game a couple more times. They said, "Wait here and we will come get you in a few minutes." A man starts talking to you and telling you about the great game in the next group of booths and asks you if you would like to try it. You might want to, but you won't, right?

You tell the man "No thanks" over and over, but he refuses to go away. You need help. Here are some ways to get it:

—Ask the person operating the game to ask the man to leave.

—Look around for a family or a woman with children who is playing at the same booth or one next to it. Walk right up and say that this man is upsetting you. They will probably wait with you until your parents return.

—Ask until you find someone who will stay with you. Do *not* try to find your family.

Avoid public restrooms. The safest ones to use are in department stores and restaurants. If you must use public bathrooms, never go alone. Take a few friends or a parent with you. If a stranger asks you to go into a bathroom with him, get away from him. Find your friends or walk toward a crowd of people at once.

Don't walk around in a daze. When you are out in public by yourself, try not to look lost or lonely. Always act like you know where you are going. Keep moving, walk briskly and act sure of yourself.

Play . . . It Smart

It should be pretty clear from the stories you read that playing alone is not a good idea. And it's not much fun either. Playing with friends is far safer—providing you play in smart places.

Stay out of . . . vacant lots, broken-down buildings, deserted woods, parking lots, fields in the middle of nowhere, alleys and streets with nothing happening. Stick to busy sections of town, parks filled with people and streets on which you know the residents . . . and they know you.

Someone should know where you are at all times. Playing it smart also means being sure that your parents know where you play. They'd be pretty upset if you told them you were going to Grant Street Park with Nick and Gordon when you actually ended up playing baseball in the schoolyard. How would they find you if they needed you?

It's very important to tell your parents when you change your plans or if you are going to be late. If you say "I'm going to Melissa's" but wind up at Becky's, call to report the switch in plans.

Do your parents know all your playmates, where they live and their telephone numbers? They should.

When you make a new friend, bring her home to meet your mother or father.

If your parents know with whom you play and the places you usually play, they will be able to find you quickly if necessary.

Who's that? If you see someone hanging around the playground or driving up and down the street on which you and your friends play, be suspicious. Study the person so that you can tell your parents something about him or his car. Tell them at once.

If you can read the license plate number, find a stick, crayon, pencil or stone and write the number in the dirt or on the sidewalk. Or you can just use your finger to trace the number in the dirt. Try to see the state name that is on the plate, but don't get close to the driver.

Coming and Going

There will be times when you are alone—maybe walking down the street to get your friend or riding your bicycle to the store.

When you are coming and going, whether you are alone or with your friends, be cautious and always be home before dark.

Don't advertise. Keep your name off your bookbag, lunchbox, jackets, shirts or anything else you wear or carry. Don't give a stranger the advantage of knowing your name.

If a stranger calls you by name (whether or not it's on your clothing or books), that doesn't automatically mean he knows you. He could have heard your name when one of your friends called to you. He could have heard your mother talking to you in the grocery store. There are many ways to find out someone's name. Handle this person the same as you would handle anyone you did not know.

Follow safe routes. A safe route should be selected with your parents for walking to and from school, practice, your friends' houses, anywhere you travel. The best routes are busy main streets and/or well-traveled roads.

Do *not* take shortcuts through unattended parking lots, empty buildings, alleys, fields or woods. Don't cut across train tracks. Wherever you go, always travel with a friend if you can.

If you want to change your route, make sure it's okay with your parents. Look for stores, office buildings or houses you could go to if you ever needed help.

Of course, you already know this: *Never hitchhike.* Not alone and not with friends.

Stick with the crowd. If you use public transportation, wait at busy bus stops. At subway or train stations, wait near token or ticket booths or stand with lots of people. Ride in crowded cars, the car with the conductor or engineer, but never in the last car. When you get off, don't hang around.

If a stranger bothers you, tell the bus driver, trainman or transit police. Do not get off until you have found help. Set off the emergency alarm if necessary.

When someone is meeting you. Here's something you can teach your parents: code words (you can also call them passwords or secret words). The word you choose must be known only by you and your parents.

If an emergency arises and they cannot pick you up as planned and no one on the list of people who always have permission to get you is available, your parents will reveal the code word to the person they send. This person will also be told that they must tell you the code word first thing. You must never ask for it or say it.

After you use a code word, change it. For example, you and a friend go to the movies during a school vacation and your father says he will pick you up at 5:15. Your code word is "birth-day cake."

At 5:15 the lady who lives at the end of your street arrives in front of the movie theater and says, "Hi, Sean, your code word is birthday cake. Your dad asked me to drive over to get you because his meeting is running late. Come on, I'll take you both home."

Obviously you now need a new code word because your friend and a neighbor know the old one. With a code word, you never have to wonder if it's okay to go with someone who says "Your mother sent me."

If no one is home. Your mother might have been delayed at the store or a doctor's appointment; you could have forgotten your key; you may feel unhappy and not want to be alone. Or you think someone has followed you. In other words, there may be some days when you want a safe place to go other than home.

Can you go to a friend's house or apartment? Does your mother have a friend who lives nearby? Can you go to a neighbor's house? Ask one of your parents to make arrangements in advance, and be sure you meet the people and visit their house so you feel comfortable going there.

At Home

Your approach and attitude toward strangers when you are home should be as careful as when you are out of the house. Use your head. Here's a chance to check your at-home safety knowledge.

Do you take these precautions automatically?
—Never tell a stranger your name or where you live.
—Never go into a house alone if something looks odd to you. Go to a neighbor's or friend's house or apartment.
—Never get on an elevator if someone makes you nervous. To get up and down safely in self-service elevators, ride alone or with people who also live in your building. When a stranger

says "Going up?" respond with "No, thanks. Go ahead. I'm waiting for my brother (mother, friend)."

If the elevator arrives at your floor and you don't like the looks of the passenger, you can say "Oops, I forgot something. Go ahead."

—Keep all doors and ground-floor windows locked.

—Answer the doorbell only if you have your parents' permission.

—Don't let anyone in no matter how pushy he is or how true his story sounds. Call a parent at work to check out what you are being told. Maybe your mother was expecting the plumber, a delivery man or the seamstress to measure the windows for curtains. Maybe not.

—When you take a telephone call, *never* admit that you are home alone. If the call is not for you, tell the caller "My mom or dad can't come to the telephone right now." Take a message and say "He/she will call you back soon." Call your mom or dad right away so that they can return the call promptly.

—Retreat quickly into the house from strangers who appear on your property. Dangerous strangers know no boundaries. They are just as likely to show up on your front lawn as they are to show up in a bus terminal, train station or at a popular campsite.

CHAPTER 12

Stranger-Proofed

Everything you have been reading and learning is prevention. Being "stranger-proofed" is the same as brushing your teeth to prevent cavities, eating nutritiously so you don't get sick or practicing water safety to avoid a serious accident.

Prevention makes good sense. If you play in sensible places and always play with and travel with your friends, unsafe strangers will have little chance to approach you.

A stranger who is planning to lure you will hardly ever do so if you are with a group, a parent or another adult. And if you ever find yourself alone, you can make it almost impossible for a stranger to bother you.

To be sure you're not confused by any of this stranger business, here's a short review.

These People Are Strangers

Whether a person is standing on your doorstep or buying a cake in a bakery, if you have never seen that person before, he or she is a *stranger*. Keep your eyes open.

A stranger is also someone you don't know well: someone you saw once or twice, but don't know his name, where he lives or anything about him.

Keep people you know only slightly on your stranger list. Even if you do know their names and may see them every day on your way to school, in a store, at the library or around the neighborhood, you don't know too much else about them. Be on guard when you see them somewhere you have never seen them before.

Any adult you meet for the first time is a stranger, too. If he introduces himself, he is a stranger. If a friend introduces him to you, he is a stranger. This new person is a stranger until your parents tell you he is a friend.

Whenever you're not sure about how to act around a grownup, whether to treat him as a friend or as a stranger, ask your parents or another adult that you trust.

Handy Responses

At this point it should be a breeze for you to decide who is a stranger and who is not. Remember, you don't ever have to answer a stranger. But suppose you want to. What do you say to a stranger who might want to trick you?

The following are some more dangerous stranger lies and questions that are designed to make you feel guilty, feel sorry for the stranger or convince you to accept whatever he or she is offering. Each encounter has responses that make getting away easier. It's not always so simple to say "No" to a grown-up, so try out these responses. Practice them with your parents, older brother or sister or your friends. Take turns being the stranger.

—A stranger says: "My daughter died. She was about your size and I don't know what to do with her clothes. They're real pretty. I'd like you to have them."

You say: "NO, THANKS." And leave the scene quickly.

—A stranger says: "I have an extra ticket for the ball game this afternoon and I don't have anyone to go with me. I just moved to town and don't know a soul. Want to keep me company?"

You say: "I'D LIKE TO, BUT I CAN'T." Or: "NO, THANKS." And leave the scene quickly.

—A stranger says: "We're making a television commercial three blocks from here and we need two more boys and one girl to be in it. Ever been on television? It's great fun. Just take a few minutes. Interested?"

You say: "NO." And leave the scene quickly.

—A stranger says: "Hey, I need to run into that store for a minute, but I can't leave all this stuff in my car. Would you sit in it so no one takes anything?"

You say: "CAN'T. HAVE TO GO." And leave the scene quickly.

—A stranger says: "I'll pay you to carry these packages into my house." Or: "I'll pay you to help me clean up my yard."

You say: "SORRY, CAN'T HELP." And get away.

—A stranger says: "I have the greatest collection of dolls (trains, cars, baseball cards) you have ever seen in your life. I'll show you. There's this very special one. Rare. You'll never see another one like it. Here, look inside my van (car, house, trailer)."

You say: "NO." Or: "HAVE TO GO. MY MOM IS WAITING RIGHT OVER THERE. SEE?" Point to any woman you see. Walk in her direction, then run to a safe place.

—A stranger says: "Looks like you could use a new bike. My boy's grown up. He doesn't need his bike anymore. It's practically new and just sitting in the garage. Come on over and I'll give it to you."

That's an easy one. You say: "NO, THANKS."

—A stranger says: "Your mother asked me to check on you while she's at work and walk you home when you're finished playing."

You say: "SHE DIDN'T SAY THAT." And find help fast.

—A stranger says: "You don't seem very happy. Look, I understand. Things are tough at your house. Your parents will appreciate you more after you've been away for a little while. Come on, let's go somewhere and talk it over."

This stranger is guessing that you had a fight with your mom and dad or that they just gave you a very heavy punishment. Everyone has trouble with a parent now and then. It's true that sometimes families have serious problems. Discussing them with a stranger is not the answer, though. You only will be taking an unnecessary risk.

Say: "NO, THANKS." And run away very fast.

—A stranger says: "I talked to your father this morning. He told me you're in one pack of trouble after another. You're not that way, are you? Let's go have some fun or a little lunch and forget about him for a while."

You say: "I DON'T BELIEVE YOU. MY FATHER NEVER SAID THAT." Don't fall into the trap of arguing with this kind of liar. Go home. Ask your father about the conversation. He will not know what you're talking about because he never saw that dishonest stranger.

—A stranger shouts: "Come on with me! I said, get over here this minute. Understand? Now! Or I'll beat you up."

Don't hesitate. Run. Never, ever stay and fight.

Yell: "HELP!" And keep yelling and running until you find help.

Stranger Alerts

Suspect any stranger who gives you the tiniest signal. Why does he want to play with me? Why does he want to take my picture? Why does he want to take me to the zoo? Why does he want to buy me a bike? Why does he think I'm so funny? So wonderful? Why is he acting as if he's my friend?

These clues will help you tell the difference between a friendly stranger who is truly a good, well-meaning person and a stranger who is pretending. Most people really do care about children—you must never forget this—but you need to be able to recognize the few that don't, and to do so quickly.

First meeting. In order to be your friend, a person must earn your trust and respect. No one can do that the very first time you meet. It takes a long time to make good friends.

Gifts and promises. Watch out for strangers who offer you money, gifts, a chance to be famous or to have a wonderful time. They are trying to buy your friendship, and everyone knows you can't buy friends.

No stranger gives presents, rewards or special treatment over and over without wanting something in return. You owe strangers and acquaintances *nothing.* Question the motive of any older person—be he your teacher, religious leader, family friend or neighbor—who spends a lot of time with you or pays more attention to you than any of your friends.

Flattery. Don't believe the stranger who tells you how great or beautiful you are or that you do things better than your friends. Ask yourself: Why is this person saying these things?

Breaking rules. You know what's right and wrong; what your parents allow you to do and what they don't. Say "No, I can't do that" to *anyone* who wants you to do something you think you should not do.

Touching. No one has the right to touch you or order you to do things you don't want to do. Don't allow it. Your body is private. It belongs *only* to you. If *anyone* touches you in a way that you don't like or that makes you feel uncomfortable, walk or run away.

Be sure to tell one of your parents what happened even if the person who touched you is your uncle or grandfather, one of your parents' friends, a friend of your older brother's or your favorite person in the whole world. You must speak up.

Secrets. If any grown-up tells you not to say a word to your parents about what happened—whatever it may be—that's your sign to tell your parents instantly. Don't keep a secret.

Threats. "I'm going to tell your mother. Now you wouldn't want her to know what I saw you doing, would you?" a stranger may ask when he discovers you playing in a place your parents told you never to go or doing something you have been forbidden to do.

This stranger is trying to scare you; he is threatening you so that you will listen to him. He wants you to do what he says, go where he tells you to go. Don't cooperate. Don't be pressured or frightened into following a stranger because you were caught. He is blackmailing you. He has no intention of telling your parents. He is bluffing.

Let him know that you realize he is trying to trap you: "I don't care if you tell." Belt it out as loudly as you can. Yell for help and run.

Authority. Often it is very difficult to figure out when a person is pretending to be a policeman, store detective, truant officer or guard. Some strangers pose as clergymen. In these cases, you may need adult help to identify such a faker.

Think twice about a person who accuses you of doing something wrong when you've done nothing. If you're puzzled by an order or don't like the way you're being treated by someone who claims to be an official, find an adult and ask him or her to check that person's identification. Real police officers and officials are never upset by such a check. In fact, they will praise you for being "stranger-wise."

Ask the person who has said you have done something wrong to call your parents. If he refuses, he could be a phony. Don't go with him; get away from him fast. Make a scene if you have to draw attention to what's happening. You can and should question grown-ups who order you around even if they are wearing uniforms and carrying badges. It is very simple to buy badges, get uniforms and turn an ordinary car into one that looks official.

The friendly twosome. A scheming stranger may not be alone. Sometimes strangers work in pairs: two men, a man and a woman, two women. A two-person team employs the same tricks and lies used by the single stranger to con you, only doubly. The pressure to go along with them may be greater. Should you experience such an encounter your willpower will be challenged.

This is a challenge you can meet by never saying "Yes" and by backing off immediately.

It's possible that you have not seen the second stranger. Before you escape from any stranger, check to be certain there is not another one blocking your way. If so, choose a different direction. If necessary, move in circles, sidestep, go forward, then backward. Just keep moving. You are wise to their tricks. And you have the advantage: You're younger and can run faster and longer than most adults.

A Special Case

Suppose a stranger grabs you and forces you into his car or van. The chances are very small that this will ever happen because you are too alert and too smart to find yourself so close to a stranger that he could get hold of you. But let's pretend anyway, so you know what to do.

First, no matter how scared you are, try to stay calm. You have to think, to plan your escape. Do not buckle your seat belt. You want to be ready to run out of the car when it stops.

The driver will have to stop eventually—at a light, at a gas station, at a restaurant. At some point he will be hungry or need a restroom. Wait. Do not jump out of a moving vehicle. And do not get out on an isolated road or near fields or any other place if there are no people, stores, houses or office buildings. You must watch for a place where you think you can get help immediately. Only you can judge if and when it is safe to make a move.

Suppose this stranger takes you and locks you in a house or building. You must be patient. At some point, and that could be a day or two away, he will leave you alone. Keep your eyes open for a chance to call the police or to run away.

Do not try to escape if there is any danger he will harm you. Wait until he slips up. That will happen. If he leaves a door or window open or leaves the phone unattended, make your call or getaway . . . fast. Run, but do so only when you are sure it is safe. Use what you have learned to get free without getting harmed. Your safety comes first.

Follow Your Instincts

Just because a grown-up is bigger and older doesn't mean he's smarter, and it doesn't mean you have to do what he says. You're a person, too. And a very important one. You have rights. You must use those rights to protect yourself.

Whether you live in a big city, a small suburb or the country, it is wise to pay attention to what's going on around you. Keep your eye on new people who appear out of nowhere or on a car that seems to be circling the area. If you stay aware, you'll notice the lady who is watching you too closely, or the two strangers who are walking too fast in your direction.

If your gut reaction—that's the feeling that comes from inside and hits you like a brick—warns you to beware, *listen to it.* You may not know exactly what is causing you to feel upset or why a person gives you the "creeps." But, if you ever feel uneasy or think you may be in danger, forget what you were taught about being polite, being "good" and obeying adults.

—Be rude! Run or walk away without answering. Don't worry about hurting a stranger's feelings. Or, tell him what you think: "That's not true." "I'm not allowed to do that."

—Say "No" and yell for help when a stranger orders you to do anything you know is wrong. When this happens to grown-ups, they say "No" and shout, and so should you. This is not the time to be a big shot or to be quietly brave. And it is certainly not the time to be weak and wishy-washy.

—Send out a signal. Passing adults will not know if you are in trouble unless you tell them. Keep in mind: Evil strangers don't necessarily look weird; they usually look very ordinary, very normal, very much like your aunt, mother, father or one of your teachers. People will think that the stranger holding on to you belongs with you. Only *you* can make sure they don't make that mistake.

—Lie or pretend. If you're like most of your friends, you're punished for lying. But if you're in a situation where a lie may help stop a grown-up from harming you, then go ahead and lie. This is one lie for which you will be praised, not punished.

Try: "My Dad's right over there." Or, go up to a woman and make believe she's your mother. Say "Hi, Mom" in a very loud voice, then whisper that the stranger over there is frightening you. Shout "Wait for me, I'm coming" and run to the closest person or group of kids.

You can tell the stranger you have to go to the bathroom

badly. You can say that you don't feel well, that you're going to vomit any second.

These suggestions will give you a start. You'll be able to think up your own lies or stories to fit the situation. If you lie, stick to your story; don't change it and don't back down until you have gotten away.

Keep yourself stranger-proofed. You have the clues that will tip you off to a stranger who might be up to no good, and you know the different ways a stranger may try to tempt you. Any stranger is going to have a pretty tough time outsmarting you.

Now that you are wise to dangerous strangers, you can certainly trust your instincts. If someone makes you feel uncomfortable, or if his actions seem fishy, make your move to get away. You'll know if you ever meet one of these people.

Tell your parents when someone or something simply doesn't feel right. Give them as much information as you can so that they can check out the problem or person for you. You are the most precious and important part of their lives. Don't go off with a stranger for any reason! Not for one minute!

Remember, strangers who plan to hurt you or take you away don't like trouble. They don't like "scenes," yelling or loud arguing. They want you to go with them peacefully, like a sleeping baby.

Don't make it easy for them. Think: No way, stranger. Not me. Give them the hardest time you can. Use every trick in this book.

You'll always know what to do, so you don't have to worry.